AIR FRYER COOKBOOK

The Complete Air Fryer Cookbook – Delicious, Quick & Easy Air Fryer Recipes For Everyone

By

William Cook

Disclaimer and Terms of Use:

Effort has been made to ensure that the information in this book is accurate and complete, however, the author and the publisher do not warrant the accuracy of the information, text and graphics contained within the book due to the rapidly changing nature of science, research, known and unknown facts and internet. The Author and the publisher do not hold any responsibility for errors, omissions or contrary interpretation of the subject matter herein. This book is presented solely for motivational and informational purposes only.

Table of Contents

Introduction

Health benefits and taste satisfying are not easy to maintain on the same lane. People around the world set new years' resolution to make it as healthy as they can. But as days go on, so goes up our craving for those deep fried wings. And when it is a gladiator battle between taste and health, taste lion always wins with his claws.

But what if we could eat those fries and still could maintain the oil input. May be it was not a truth for our ancestors but in this era of future, impossible is just a myth. And here I am going to tell a taste story of an easy to use device with very basic cooking principle. The story is about the Air Fryer.

This very effective device cooks the finest and makes it crispy with health assurance. So the recipes I am going to describe in this book are going to help you keep track of your health meter. Actually I am going to write more books relating this magic box cooker. This is the first one and I hope you are going to love the recipes and support the book.

What Is an Air Fryer?

It is a very straight forward mechanism of heat circulation is the heart of this device. In an air fryer there is a heat coil above the removable food container. The container has small holes in its bottom. There is a fan over the heat coil. The hollow inner body wall of the device is designed in such a way that when the coil is heated and the fan runs, the hot air circulates though the food. Thus, the food is well cooked. To maintain the air pressure, there is a small pass way on the top of the device which is controlled by valves. The body of this device is heat insulated. So the heat transmitted by the coil is used to the most to cook your delights.

Though it is a new concept of cooking but it is a very effective one. The function is also very simple but the outcome is impressive. Its easy mechanism makes it energy efficient. In deep fryer where the surrounding oil cooks the food, here the surrounding hot air does the job. Thus, the food is healthy and tasty at the same time. Also, the food is very fresh to eat for the air circulation process.

How to Use Your Air Fryer

Using an air fryer is the most convenient and easy thing to do. Simply take the food container out, place the food, attach the container as it was before and set the timer. The main benefit here is that whichever dish you are preparing you will be needed smallest amount of cooking oil. It is widely advertised and tested that most of the frying in Air Fryer needs as little as a spoon of oil. You can just do required seasoning to your dish and spray little oil on it evenly, take it in the fryer and give required time. You can find required time in every dish that I included in my book. As it is easy to carry, you can take it anywhere you like. You can even use it in your recreational vehicle to serve your hot delights. You can use it anywhere as long as you can find a useable power source. Taking care of this device is not even can be considered as a matter. The food container is easy to wash and rest of the device doesn't even need any taking care.

This device has a wide range of usability. It can make your French fries crispy outside and perfectly moist inside. It can even cook your steak and fish. You will find me talking about different recipes using it in this book all the time. One thing I can assure you that if you are thinking to invest on an air fryer and a good air fryer recipe book, it will give you the most outcome out of your bucks.

The Benefits of Air Fryer

Air Fryer is all in one in the sense of benefits. It can cook in the least amount of time needed. The foods which are served by making in this device are very well cooked and delicious without being oily. Health conscious people find it very hard to maintain the oil in food. You can use many time consuming process to control your oil intake but the best you will find in an air fryer. As I have spoken earlier, an air fryer takes very less amount of oil to cook the food. So instead of frying things in oil, you can have the same crispy taste without spending on oil and your health.

The other benefit is that it takes very less time to cook the meal. Approximately half of the time an oven takes. So it is very effective in this manner. It is also efficient in manner of heat use. It is designed in a way that most of the heat produced by the coil is used to cook the food. Heat goes through the food and cooks it evenly. One more benefit in effectiveness is that when it passes some air out to maintain air pressure, it actually filters the air. So you don't have to be suffocated while you cook. It guarantees a good environment outside. It is actually effective in every manner as we think.

You can easily clean this device. The main part to clean here is the food container. You can remove it and wash it as a normal pan. As the rest of the devise does not come in touch with the food so there is no need to clean the other parts.

Its portability makes it beyond a home appliance. You can take it with you to anywhere. You just need power and 5 minutes to make your food ready. It is a life saver in this case. So, if the next time it's late at night and you are craving for some spicy food, you can have it before you know that you have cooked.

What You Will Find in My Book

As I have said earlier air fryer has so much to offer and it's hard for me to write all entire finger licking recipes in one book. So you are going to have a well around quick recipes in this book for keep you moving all day long. There will be recipes for breakfast, lunch and dinner. I think dinner should be most versatile and every day should be a food safari. In my book you will also find recipes for chicken, pork, beef & turkey, and seafood.

Dinner is not fulfilled without appetizers, side dishes and desserts. So there are a decent amount of side dish, appetizers and snacks, dessert and bread recipes.

The recipes you will find here are organized to the most effective way. You will find in a very short time that it will become your menu for your home restaurant. Each recipe has its preparation time mentioned. I will highly recommend you to try all the recipes. Each one has its own pride in this taste jungle.

Measurement Conversions

US Dry Volume Measurements

1/16 teaspoon	Dash
1/8 teaspoon	Pinch
3 teaspoons	1 tablespoon
1/8 cup	2 tablespoons (1 standard coffee scoop)
1/4 cup	4 tablespoons
1/3 cup	5 tablespoons plus 1 teaspoon
1/2 cup	8 tablespoons
3/4 cup	12 tablespoons
1 cup	16 tablespoons
1 pound	16 ounces

US liquid volume measurements

8 Fluid ounces	1 Cup
1 Pint	2 Cups (16 fluid ounces)
1 Quart	2 Pints (4 cups)
1 Gallon	4 Quarts (16 cups)

US to Metric Conversions

1/5 teaspoon	1 ml (ml stands for milliliter, one thousandth of a liter)
1 teaspoon	5 ml
1 tablespoon	15 ml
1 fluid oz.	30 ml
1/5 cup	50 ml
1 cup	240 ml
2 cups (1 pint)	470 ml
4 cups (1 quart)	.95 liter
4 quarts (1 gal)	3.8 liters
1 oz.	28 grams
1 pound	454 grams

Metric to US Conversions

1 milliliter	1/5 teaspoon
5 ml	1 teaspoon
15 ml	1 tablespoon
30 ml	1 fluid oz.
100 ml	3.4 fluid oz.
240 ml	1 cup
1 liter	34 fluid oz.
1 liter	4.2 cups
1 liter	2.1 pints
1 liter	1.06 quarts
1 liter	.26 gallon
1 gram	.035 ounce
100 grams	3.5 ounces
500 grams	1.10 pounds
1 kilogram	2.205 pounds
1 kilogram	35 oz.

Temperature Conversions

Fahrenheit	Celsius	Gas Mark
275° F	140° C	gas mark 1-cool
300° F	150° C	gas mark 2
325° F	165° C	gas mark 3-very moderate
350° F	180° C	gas mark 4-moderate
375° F	190° C	gas mark 5
400° F	200° C	gas mark 6-moderately hot
425° F	220° C	gas mark 7- hot
450° F	230° C	gas mark 9
475° F	240° C	gas mark 10- very hot

Abbreviations:

Cooking Abbreviation(s)	Unit of Measurement
C, c	cup
g	gram
kg	kilogram
L, l	liter
lb	pound
mL, ml	milliliter
oz	ounce
pt	pint
t, tsp	teaspoon
T, TB, Tbl, Tbsp	tablespoon

Breakfast Recipes

Air Fryer Donuts Recipe

Total Time: 10 minutes
Servings: 8 donuts + 8 holes

Ingredients

- 1 can Pillsbury grinds flaky layers biscuits (8 biscuits; can use generic brands as well — I used Hy-Vee biscuits)
- 3 tablespoons melted butter
- 1/3 cup granulated sugar
- 1/2 to 1 teaspoon cinnamon
- 4 tablespoons dark brown sugar (try to remove any clumps)
- Pinch of allspice

Directions

1. Put sugar, cinnamon, brown sugar, and allspice together in a little (cereal or soup sized) bowl and keep aside.
2. Remove biscuits from jar (do not flatten) and use a 1-inch circle biscuit cutter to cut the circles out of the center of each biscuit.
3. Now air fry the DONUTS at 350 degrees Fahrenheit for 5 minutes (some fried 4 at a time), and air fry the HOLES at 350 degrees F for just 3 minutes (some fried all 8 holes at once).
4. When each batch of donuts and holes comes out of the fryer, get a pastry brush to paint butter over the entire surface of each donut and hole.
5. After that each donut and hole is painted with butter, drop into the bowl with the sugar mixture and coat fully with the mixture. Then gently shake off excess.
6. Now serve donuts and holes warm.

Hash Brown Recipe

Prep Time: 15 minutes | Cook Time: 15 minutes | Total Time: 30 minutes
Serves: 8 pieces

Ingredients

- 4 peeled and finely grated large potatoes
- 2 tablespoons corn flour
- Salt – to taste
- Pepper powder – to taste
- 2 teaspoons of Chili flakes
- Onion Powder – 1 teaspoon (optional)
- Vegetable Oil – 1 + 1 teaspoon
- 1 teaspoon of Garlic Powder (optional)

Instructions

1. Steep the shredded potatoes in cold water. Pull out the water. Repeat the step to drain excess starch from potatoes.
2. In a non-stick pan heat 1 tablespoon of vegetable oil and bake shredded potatoes till cooked slightly for 3-4 minutes.
3. Keep it to cool down and transfer the potatoes to a plate.
4. Put corn flour, pepper, salt, garlic and onion powder and chili flakes and mix together quickly.
5. Spread over the plate and mix it gently with your fingers.
6. Keep it in refrigerator for 20 minutes.
7. Preheat air fryer at 180C
8. Then take out the refrigerated potato and divide it into equal pieces with a knife
9. Brush the wire jar of the air fryer with little oil
10. Place the hash brown pieces in the basket and fry for 15 minutes at 180C
11. Take out the basket and turn over the hash browns at 6 minutes so that they are air fried gently on the both sides.
12. Serve it warm with ketchup

Cinnamon Rolls

Preparation Time: 2 hours | Cooking Time: 20 minutes | Total Time: 2 hours 20 minutes
Serves: 8

Ingredients

- ¾ cup brown sugar
- 1½ tablespoons ground cinnamon
- 1 pound frozen bread dough, thawed
- ¼ cup butter, melted and cooled

Cream Cheese Glaze

- 4 ounces cream cheese, softened
- 2 tablespoons butter, softened
- 1¼ cups powdered sugar
- ½ teaspoon vanilla

Instructions

1. At first leave the bread dough come to room temperature on the counter. On a floured surface roll the dough into a 13-inch by 11-inch rectangle. Then position the rectangle so the 13-inch portion is facing you. Brush the melted butter all over the dough surface, letting a 1-inch border uncovered along with the edge farthest away from you.
2. Then mix the brown sugar and cinnamon in a small bowl. Sprinkle the combination evenly over the buttered dough, leaving the 1-inch border uncovered. Roll the dough into a log beginning with the edge nearest to you. Roll the dough tightly, just make sure to roll evenly and push out any air pockets. When you reach to the uncovered edge of the dough, press the dough onto the roll to seal it together.
3. Cut the log into 8 pieces, piecing slowly with a sawing motion so you don't flatten the dough. Now turn the slices on their sides and cover with a neat kitchen towel. Let the rolls sit in the hottest part of your kitchen for 1½ to 2 hours to rise.
4. For making the glaze, place the cream cheese and butter in a microwave-safe bowl. Soften the mixture in the microwave for 30 seconds at a time until it is easy to stir. Gradually mix the powdered sugar and stir to combine. Add the vanilla extract and whisk until smooth. Set aside.
5. As the rolls have risen, pre-heat the air fryer to 350ºF.
6. Switch 4 of the rolls to the air fryer basket. Air-fry for 5 minutes. Turn the rolls over and air-fry for another 4 minutes. Do again with the remaining 4 rolls.
7. Leave the rolls cool for a couple of minutes before glazing. Spread a large amount of dollops of cream cheese glaze on top of the warm cinnamon rolls, allowing some of the glaze to drip down the side of the rolls. Serve warm and enjoy!

Frittata Recipe

Cooking Time: 10 minutes
Servings: 1

Ingredients

- 3 eggs
- ½ Italian sausage
- 4 cherry tomatoes (in half)
- 1 tablespoon olive oil
- Chopped parsley
- Grand Padano cheese (or parmesan)
- Salt/Pepper

Instructions

1. Preheat the Air Fryer to 360 degrees.
2. Put the cherry tomatoes and sausage in the baking accessory and cook at 360 degrees for 5 minutes.
3. In a small bowl, whisk the remaining ingredients together.
4. Keep aside the baking accessory from the Air Fryer and add the egg mixture, making sure it is even. Bake it for another 5 minutes.

Perfect Cinnamon Toast

Prep Time: 5 minutes | Cook Time: 5 minutes | Total Time: 10 minutes
Serves: 6 servings

Ingredients

- 12 pieces Bread, whole wheat is great
- 1 stick Salted Butter, room temperature
- ½ cup Sugar
- 1 ½ teaspoons Ground Cinnamon
- 1 ½ teaspoons Vanilla Extract
- 4-6 cranks Fresh Ground Black Pepper, optional

Instructions

1. Crush softened butter with a fork or back of spoon and put in sugar, cinnamon, pepper and vanilla.
2. Blend to completely combine.
3. Spread on bread, making sure to fully cover the whole surface.
4. Place as many pieces fit into your Air Fryer.
5. Heat it at 400 degrees Fahrenheit for 5 minutes.
6. Get it out from the Air Fryer and cut diagonally.

Tofu Scramble

Prep Time: 5 minutes | Total Time: 35 minutes | Cook Time: 30 minutes
Serves: 3 servings

Ingredients

- 1 block tofu chopped into 1" pieces
- 2 tablespoons soy sauce
- 1 tablespoon olive oil
- 1 teaspoon turmeric
- ½ teaspoon garlic powder
- ½ teaspoon onion powder
- ½ cup chopped onion
- 2 ½ cups chopped red potato 1" cubes, 2-3 potatoes
- 1 tablespoon olive oil
- 4 cups broccoli florets

Instructions

1. At first put together the tofu, olive oil, soy sauce, turmeric, garlic powder, onion powder, and onion in a medium sized bowl. Keep aside to marinate.
2. Then in a separate small bowl, keep the potatoes in the olive oil, and air fry it at 400F for 15 minutes, shaking once around 7-8 minutes into cooking.
3. Shake the potatoes again, then add the tofu, keeping any leftover marinate. Set the tofu and potatoes to cook at 370F for 15 more minutes, and begin the air fryer.
4. While the tofu is cooking, put the broccoli in the reserved marinate. If there isn't enough to get it all over the broccoli, add an extra bit of soy sauce. Dry broccoli is not your companion. When there are 5 minutes of cooking time remaining, add the broccoli to the air fryer.

Sausage and Cheese Wraps

Prep Time: 5 minutes | Cook Time: 3 minutes x 2 batches = 6 minutes
Serves: 1

Ingredients

- Heat N' Serve Sausages – 8
- 2 Pieces of American Cheese cut into ¼'s
- 1 Can of 8 count Refrigerated Crescent Roll Dough
- Wooden Skewers – 8
- Ketchup, Syrup or BBQ for dipping

Instructions

1. On a flat surface, move apart Crescent Rolls.
2. Open the Sausages.
3. Cut out the Cheese.
4. Put One Crescent Roll on the surface, unrolled.
5. Try to work from Wide Triangle to tip of the triangle.
6. Then add some sausage and cheese strip to the widest part of the crescent roll.
7. Now pull each end over sausage and cheese.
8. Roll and tuck the other existing of the dough until you reach the edge of the triangle.
9. Please make sure to pinch all the dough.
10. Place up to 4 of these doughes in Air Fryer.
11. Select the 380° temperature for 3 minutes (or 4 until it gets golden brown).
12. Remove and add in skewer.
13. And then tray and serve with BBQ, Ketchup or Syrup for dunking.

Homemade Sausage Rolls

Prep Time: 20 minutes | Cook Time: 25 minutes | Total Time: 45 minutes
Servings: 4

Ingredients

- 225g Plain Flour
- 100g Butter
- Olive oil – 1 tablespoon
- Sausage meat – 300g
- 1 Medium Egg beaten
- 1 Tsp Mustard
- 1 Tsp parsley
- Pepper & salt

Instructions

1. Begin it by making your pastry. Put the flour, the seasoning and the butter into a mixing bowl and make the rubbing in method, rub the fat into the flour until you have a combination that resembles bread crumbs. Add the olive oil and a small amount of water (a bit at a time) and using your hands make the mixture into flaky dough. Knead the pastry as you mix it together so that it becomes soft and smooth.
2. Then roll out the pastry onto a worktop and create a square size of pastry. Using a teaspoon (or your fingers) rub the mustard into the pastry. Put the sausage meat in the center point and brush the edges of the pastry with egg. Roll up the sausage rolls and then divide into parts. Brush the tops and sides of the sausage rolls with more eggs.
3. Size the top of the sausage rolls with a knife so that they have the chance to spread.
4. Heat in the Air fryer at 160c for 20 minutes and then for a further 5 minutes at 200c so that you can have that lovely crunchy pastry.
5. Serve and enjoy.

Vegan Beignets

Cooking Time: 20 Minutes
Serve: 24 beignets

Ingredients

For The Powdered Baking Blend

- 1 cup Whole Earth Sweetener Baking Blend
- 1 teaspoon organic corn starch

For The Proofing

- 1 cup full-fat coconut milk from a can
- 3 tablespoons powdered baking blend
- 1 1/2 teaspoons active baking yeast

For The Dough

- 2 tablespoons melted coconut oil
- 2 tablespoons aquafaba (the drained water from a can of chickpeas)
- 2 teaspoons vanilla
- 3 cups unbleached white flour (with a little extra to sprinkle on the cutting board for later)

Instructions

1. Preheat your air fryer to 390 degrees. Depending on the size of your air fryer you can put 3 to 6 beignets in at a time.
2. Cook for 3 minutes on one side. Flip them, then cook another 2 minutes. Since air fryers vary, you may need to cook yours another minute or two for them to get golden brown.
3. Sprinkle liberally with the powdered baking blend you made in the beginning and enjoy!
4. Continue cooking in batches until they are all cooked.

Air-Fried Burgers

Prep Time: 10 minutes | Cook Time: 10 minutes | Total time: 20 minutes
Serves: 4

Ingredients

- 1 Tablespoon Worcestershire sauce
- 1 teaspoon maggi sauce
- Few drops liquid smoke
- ½ teaspoon garlic powder
- ½ teaspoon onion powder
- ½ teaspoon salt substitutes
- ½ teaspoon ground black pepper
- ½ teaspoon dried oregano
- 1 teaspoon dried parsley
- 1 pound(s) uncooked 93% extra-lean ground beef

Instructions

1. Spray the upper Actifry tray and set aside. If you use a basket-type fryer, no need to spray the basket. For basket-types, cooking temperature will be 180 C / 350 F.
2. Take a small bowl and mix together all the seasoning items.
3. Take the ground beef in a large bowl.
4. Mix well keeping in mind that overworking the meat leads to tough burgers.
5. Divide the beef mixture into 4, and shape the patties. Make an indent in the centre of each one to prevent the patties bunching up in the middle.
6. Put tray in Actifry and spray tops of patties lightly.
7. Cook 10 minutes for medium and longer to your cooking doneness expectation. There is no need to turn the patties.
8. Now serve with bun and side dishes you like.

Bourbon Bacon Burger

Total Time: 29 minutes
Serves: 2

Ingredients

- Bourbon 1 tbsp.
- Brown sugar 2 tbsp.
- 3 strips maple bacon, cut in half
- ¾ pound ground beef (80% lean)
- 1 tablespoon minced onion
- 2 tablespoons BBQ sauce
- ½ teaspoon salt
- freshly ground black pepper
- 2 slices Colby Jack cheese (or Monterey Jack)
- 2 Kaiser rolls
- lettuce and tomato, for serving
- Zesty Burger Sauce:
- 2 tablespoons BBQ sauce
- 2 tablespoons mayonnaise
- ¼ teaspoon ground paprika
- freshly ground black pepper

Instructions

1. At the beginning pre-heat the air fryer to 390ºF and pour a little water into the bottom of the air fryer rack. (This will help remove the grease that drips into the bottom drawer from heating and smoking.)
2. Mix the bourbon and brown sugar in a small bowl. Place the bacon strips in the air fryer basket and sweep it with the brown sugar mixture. Air-fry at 390ºF for 4 minutes. Turn over the bacon over, brush with more brown sugar and air-fry at 390ºF for an additional 4 minutes until it gets crispy.
3. While the bacon is cooking, start to make the burger patties. Combine the ground beef, BBQ sauce, onion salt and pepper in a big bowl. Mix together thoroughly with your hands and size the meat into 2 patties.
4. Transfer the burger patties to the air fryer basket and air-fry the burgers at 370ºF for 15 to 20 minutes, depending on how you want your burger cooked (15 minutes for rare to medium-rare; 20 minutes for well-done). Turn the burgers over halfway through the cooking process.
5. By the time burgers are air-frying, make the burger sauce by mixing the BBQ sauce, mayonnaise, paprika and freshly ground black pepper to taste in a bowl.

6. When the burgers are cooked to your liking, top each patty with a slice of Colby Jack cheese and air-fry for an additional minute, just to melt down the cheese. Spread the sauce on the inside of the Kaiser rolls, keep the burgers on the rolls, top with the bourbon bacon, lettuce and tomato and enjoy!

Chicken Quesadillas Recipe

Total Time: 20 minutes
Servings: 1

Ingredients

- Soft Taco Shells
- Chicken Fajita Strips
- Sliced green peppers ½ cup
- Sliced onions ½ cup.
- Shredded Mexican Cheese
- Salsa (optional)
- Sour Cream (optional)

Instructions

1. Firstly, preheat Air Fryer on 370 for about 3 minutes.
2. Spray vegetable oil lightly on the pan
3. Place 1 soft and firm taco shell in pan.
4. Place shredded cheese on shell. (You can use as much as you'd like.)
5. Lay out fajita chicken strips so they are in a single layer.
6. Keep your onions and green peppers on top of your chicken.
7. Insert more shredded cheese.
8. Place another soft taco shell on top and spray lightly with vegetable oil. (Sometimes I put the rack that came with the air fryer on top of the shell to hold it in place. If you don't, the fan will suck it up.)
9. Set timer for 4 minutes.
10. Turn it over carefully with large spatula.
11. Spray lightly with vegetable oil and put rack on top of shell to hold it in place.
12. Watch timer for 4 minutes.
13. If it's not crispy enough for you, keep it in for a couple of extra minutes.
14. Remove and cut it into 4 slices or 6 slices.
15. Serve with Salsa and sour cream if wanted. Enjoy!

Chick-Fil-A Nuggets

Prep Time: 15 minutes | Cook Time: 8 minutes | Total Time: 23 minutes
Serves: 6 servings

Ingredients

- Dill pickle juice 1 cup
- Boneless skinless chicken breasts 1 lb cut into pieces about 1 inch in size
- 1 egg
- Milk 1 cup
- 1½ cups flour
- Powdered sugar 3 tbsp
- 2 tsp salt
- 1½ tsp pepper
- ½ tsp paprika
- Olive oil spritz

Instructions

1. Put chicken chunks to pickle juice and marinate in the refrigerator for about 30 minutes.
2. Keep milk and egg together and set aside.
3. Mix the dry ingredients and stir set aside.
4. Preheat air fryer at 370.
5. Remove the chicken from refrigerator, drain and place each into the dry mixture, to the liquid mixture and back to the dry making sure it is well coated, making sure to shake off excess.
6. Cook it in a single layer of chicken for 8 minutes or till it gets golden brown, flipping and adding olive oil at the halfway mark.
7. Serve with your favorite dipping sauce.

Leftover Turkey & Cheese Calzone

Prep Time: 10 minutes | Cook Time: 10 minutes | Total Time: 20 minutes
Servings: 4

Ingredients

- 4 Tbsp homemade tomato sauce
- Leftover Turkey brown meat shredded
- Cheddar chase 100 g
- 25g Mozzarella Cheese grated
- 25g Back Bacon diced
- 1 Large Egg beaten
- Tomatos puree 1 Tbsp.
- Basil 1 Tsp
- Oregano 1 Tsp
- 1 Tsp Thyme
- Salt & Pepper

Instructions

1. Preheat the Air Fryer to 180c.
2. Begin it by rolling out your pizza dough so that they are all the size of small pizzas. In a small mixing bowl keep together all the seasonings as well as the tomato sauce and puree.
3. Using a cooking brush to add a layer of tomato sauce to your pizza bases making sure that it doesn't actually touch the sides with a 1cm space.
4. Then layer up your pizza with your turkey, bacon and cheese to one side.
5. The 1cm gap around your pizza base and using your cooking brush again, brush with egg. Fold your pizza base over so that it resembles an uncooked Cornish pasty and all area that is now visible of the pizza dough to be brushed with more egg.
6. Put the Air Fryer for 10 minutes at 180c.
7. Serve.

Air Fryer Chick-Fil-A Chicken Sandwich

Prep Time: 10 minutes | Cook Time: 16 minutes | Total Time: 26 minutes
Servings: 2

Ingredients

- 2 Boneless/Skinless Chicken Breasts (Pounded)
- 1/2 cup of Dill Pickle Juice
- 2 Eggs
- 1/2 cup of Milk
- 1 cup All Purpose Flour
- 2 Tablespoons of Powdered Sugar
- 1 teaspoon of Paprika
- 1 teaspoon of Sea Salt
- 1/2 teaspoon of Freshly Ground Black Pepper
- 1/2 teaspoon of Garlic Powder
- 1/4 teaspoon of Ground Celery Seed ground
- 1 Tablespoon of Extra Virgin Olive Oil extra virgin
- 1 Oil Mister
- 4 Hamburger Buns toasted or buttered
- 8 Dill Pickle Chips or more

Spicy Option

- 1/4 teaspoon of Cayenne Pepper for spicy sandwiches

Instructions

1. Take chicken into a Ziploc Bag and pound. Each whole piece should be the in same thickness, about 1/2 inches thick.
2. Cut chicken into two or three pieces depending on size.
3. Take chicken again into Ziploc bag and pour in pickle juice. Refrigerate for at least 30 minutes.
4. Take a medium bowl and beat egg with the milk in it.
5. Take another bowl, combine flour with all spices.
6. After that coat chicken with egg mixture followed by flour mixture, making sure pieces are completely coated. Take extra flour off with gentle shake.
7. Spray the bottom of your Air Fryer basket with Oil.
8. Transfer chicken into air fryer and spray the chicken with Oil.
9. Air fry at 340 degrees for 6 minutes. Carefully flip the chicken and spray with Oil. Cook for another 6 minutes.
10. Raise the temperature to 400 degrees and cook for more two minutes on each side.
11. Serve on buttered and toasted buns with your preferred sauce or mayonnaise.

Air Fryer Hot Dogs

Prep Time: 3 minutes | Cook Time: 7 minutes | Total Time: 10 minutes
Servings: 2

Ingredients

- 2 hot dogs
- 2 hot dog buns
- 2 tablespoons of grated cheese if desired

Directions

- Preheat your air fryer. Temperature should be 390 degrees for about 4 minutes.
- Place two hot dogs into the air fryer and air fry for about 5 minutes.
- Take the hot dog out of the air fryer.
- Transfer the hot dog on a bun with cheese (if desired).
- Take prepared hot dog into the air fryer, and cook for another 2 minutes.

Dinner

Lemon Pepper Chicken in the Air Fryer

Prep Time: 3 minutes | Cook Time: 15 minutes | Total Time: 18 minutes
Servings: 1

Ingredients

- 1 Chicken Breast
- 2 Lemons rind and juice
- 1 Tablespoon Chicken Seasoning
- 1 Teaspoon Garlic Puree
- Handful Black Peppercorns
- Salt & Pepper

Instructions

1. Preheat the air fryer to 180c.
2. Set up your cooking materials. Place a large sheet of silver foil on the work top and add to it all the seasonings and the lemon rind.
3. Lay out your chicken breasts onto a chopping board and trim off any fatty bits or any little bones that are still there. Then season each side with salt and pepper. Rub the chicken seasoning into both sides so that it is slightly a different color.
4. Place it in the silver foil sheet and rub it well so that it is fully seasoned.
5. Then seal it up very tight so that it can't breathe as this will help get the flavor into it.
6. Then give it a slap with a rolling pin so that it will flatten it out and release more flavor.
7. Place it in the air fryer for 15 minutes and check to see if it is fully cooked in the middle before serving.

Healthy Air Fried Chicken Tenders

Prep Time: 10 minutes | Cook Time: 10 minutes | Total Time: 20 minutes
Serves: 2

Ingredients

- 12oz of Chicken Breasts
- 1 Egg White
- 1/8 Cup Flour
- 35g Panko Bread Crumbs
- Salt and Pepper

Instructions

1. First, Trim chicken breast of any excess fat and cut into tenders. Season each side with salt and pepper.
2. Then, Dip chicken tenders into flour, then egg whites, then panko bread crumbs.
3. After that, Load into air fryer basket and spray with olive spray.
4. Finally, Cook at 350 degrees for about 10 minutes or until cooked through

Easy Air Fryer KFC Chicken Strips

Prep Time: 10 minutes | Cook Time: 12 minutes | Total Time: 22 minutes
Servings: 8

Ingredients

- 1 Chicken Breast (chopped into strips)
- 15 ml Desiccated Coconut
- 15 ml Plain Oats
- 5 ml KFC Spice Blend
- 75 ml Bread Crumbs
- 50 g Plain Flour
- 1 Small Egg beaten
- Salt
- Pepper

Instructions

1. Chop up the chicken breast into strips.
2. In a bowl add the coconut, oats, KFC spice blend, bread crumbs and salt and pepper.
3. In another bowl have the egg and in another take the plain flour.
4. Put your strips in the plain flour first. Then in the egg and finally in the spicy layer.
5. Put the Airfryer at 180c and cook for 8 minutes. Then cook for a further 4 minutes on 160c so that the chicken is cooked in the center.
6. Serve hot.

Pickle-Brined Fried Chicken

Total Time: 47 minutes
Serves: 4

Ingredients

- 4 chicken legs with bone & skin, cut into drumsticks and thighs (about 3½ pounds)
- pickle juice from a 24-ounce jar of kosher dill pickles
- ½ cup flour
- freshly ground black pepper and salt
- 2 eggs
- 2 tablespoons of vegetable or canola oil
- 1 cup fine breadcrumbs
- 1 teaspoon salt
- 1 teaspoon freshly ground black pepper
- ½ teaspoon ground paprika
- ⅛ teaspoon cayenne pepper
- vegetable or canola oil in a spray bottle

Instructions

1. Take the chicken in a dish and pour the pickle juice over the top. Cover and transfer the chicken to the refrigerator to brine in the pickle juice for 3 to 8 hours.
2. Before Cooking, remove the chicken from the refrigerator to let it come to room temperature. In the meanwhile you set up a dredging station. Take the flour in a shallow dish and season well with salt and freshly ground black pepper. Whisk the eggs and vegetable oil together in another shallow dish. In another shallow dish, combine the breadcrumbs, salt, pepper, paprika and cayenne pepper.
3. Pre-heat the Airfryer to 370ºF.
4. Remove the chicken from pickle brine and soak with a clean kitchen towel. Dredge each piece of chicken in the flour followed by dipping it into the egg mixture. Finally press it into the breadcrumb mixture to coat all sides of the chicken evenly. Place these pieces on a plate or baking sheet and spray each piece all over with vegetable or canola oil.
5. Air-fry the pieces in two separate batches. Place two chicken thighs and two drumsticks into the air fryer basket. Fry for 10 minutes. Then, turn the chicken pieces over and air fry for another 10 minutes. Remove the chicken pieces and let them rest on plate without covering. Repeat with the second batch of chicken.
6. Lower the temperature to 340ºF. Place the first batch of chicken on top of the second batch already in the basket and air fry for an additional 7 minutes. Serve immediately.

Air-Fried Buttermilk Chicken

Total time: 18 minutes
Serves: 1

Ingredients

- 800g chicken thighs with skin and bone

Marinade

- 2 cups of buttermilk
- 2 teaspoons of salt
- 2 teaspoons of black pepper
- 1 teaspoon of cayenne pepper (I used paprika powder)

Seasoned Flour

- 2 cups of all-purpose flour
- 1 tablespoon of baking powder
- 1 tablespoon of garlic powder
- 1 tablespoon of paprika powder
- 1 teaspoon salt

Instructions

1. Clean the chicken with water and pat dry with tissue.
2. Take chicken pieces, black pepper, paprika and salt in a large bowl and mix well to coat. Pour buttermilk over the spice mixed chicken until it is coated. Refrigerate for at least 6 hours or overnight.
3. Preheat airfryer. Temperature should be 180c.
4. In another bowl, combine flour, baking powder, paprika and salt and pepper. Take 1 piece of chicken at a time from the buttermilk and dredge in seasoned flour. Shake off any excess flour and place to a plate.
5. Place chicken one layer on the fryer basket, skin side up, and include the basket into the airfryer. Air fry for 8 minutes. Pull out the tray, turn over chicken pieces, and set timer for another 10 minutes.
6. Allow to drain on paper towels and then serve.

Air Fryer Roast Chicken

Total time: 50 minutes
Serves: 1

Ingredients

- pound whole chicken
- Ingredients for dry rub recipe or your own seasonings

Instructions

1. Clean and dry chicken.
2. Sprinkle with dry rub or own seasonings.
3. Spray fry basket with cooking spray and take chicken into the basket with the legs facing down.
4. Roast the chicken for 330 degrees Fahrenheit for 30 minutes.
5. Flip chicken over.
6. Roast for another 20 more minutes at 330 degrees Fahrenheit or until the chicken is well cooked with 165 degrees internal temperature.

Chicken Parmesan in the Air Fryer

Total Time: 30 Minutes
Serves: 1

Ingredients

- 2 (each about 8 oz) chicken breast, sliced in half to make 4 cutlets
- 6 tablespoons seasoned breadcrumbs (I used whole wheat, gluten-free also can be used)
- 2 tablespoons grated of Parmesan cheese
- 1 tablespoon of butter, melted (or olive oil)
- 6 tablespoons reduced fat mozzarella cheese
- 1/2 cup marinara
- cooking spray

Instructions

1. Preheat the air fryer at 360F° for 9 minutes. Spray the basket lightly with spray.
2. Mix breadcrumbs and parmesan cheese in a bowl. Take the butter in another bowl to melt.
3. Lightly spread the butter onto the chicken, and then dip into the breadcrumb mixture.
4. Place 2 pieces in the basket of the preheated airfryer and spray the top with oil.
5. Cook for 6 minutes, turn over and top each with 1 table spoon sauce and 1 1/2 table spoon of shredded mozzarella cheese.
6. Cook for 3 more minutes till the cheese is completely melted.
7. Set the 2 pieces aside and keep warm, repeat the process with the remaining 2 pieces.

KFC Popcorn Chicken in the Air Fryer

Prep Time: 10 minutes | Cook Time: 12 minutes | Total time: 22 minutes
Servings: 12

Ingredients

- 1 chicken breast
- 2 ml of KFC spice blend
- 60 ml of bread crumbs
- 1 small egg beaten
- 50 g plain flour
- Salt & pepper

Instructions

1. In the food processor blend your chicken till it resembles minced chicken.
2. Take flour in a bowl and a second bowl with your beaten egg. In another bowl mix together your KFC spice blend, your salt and pepper and then the bread crumbs.
3. Then make minced chicken into balls and roll in the flour, the egg and then the spiced bread crumbs.
4. Place in the balls in the airfryer at 180c for 10-12 minutes or until cooked in the middle.

Air-Fried Turkey Breast with Maple Mustard Glaze

Total Time: 59 minutes
Serves: 6

Ingredients

- 2 teaspoons of olive oil
- 5-pound whole turkey breast
- 1 teaspoon of dried thyme
- ½ teaspoon of dried sage
- ½ teaspoon of smoked paprika
- 1 teaspoon of salt
- ½ teaspoon of freshly ground black pepper
- ¼ cup of maple syrup
- 2 tablespoons of Dijon mustard
- 1 tablespoon of butter

Instructions

1. Pre heat air fryer. Temperature should be 350ºF.
2. Brush the olive oil all over the turkey breast well.
3. Mix the thyme, sage, paprika, salt and pepper and rub the outside of the turkey breast with the spice mixture.
4. Place the seasoned turkey breast to the air fryer basket and fry at 350ºF for 25 minutes. Turn the turkey breast on its side and fry for another 12 minutes. Then Turn the turkey breast on the opposite side and fry for another 12 minutes. The internal temperature of the turkey breast should reach to 165ºF when fully cooked.
5. While the turkey is air-frying, mix the maple syrup, mustard and butter in a small saucepan. When the cooking is done, take the turkey breast to an upright position and brush the mixture all over the turkey. Air-fry for another 5 minutes, till the skin is nicely browned and crispy. Let the turkey rest, loosely covered with foil, for at least 5 minutes before slicing.
6. Serve.

The Ultimate Air Fryer Burgers

Prep Time: 14 minutes | Cook Time: 45 minutes | Total Time: 59 minutes
Servings: 4

Ingredients

- 300g Mixed Mince pork and beef
- Onion
- 1 Tsp of Garlic Puree
- 1 Tsp of Tomato Puree
- 1 Tsp of Mustard
- 1 Tsp of Basil
- 1 Tsp of Mixed Herbs
- Salt
- Pepper
- 25g Cheddar Cheese
- 4 Bread Buns
- Salad for burger topping

Instructions

1. In a mixing bowl take the mince and seasoning to mix well.
2. Shape into four medium sized burgers and place it into the cooking tray of the airfryer.
3. Cook at 200c for 25 minutes and then check. Then cook them for another 20 minutes on 180c.
4. Add salad, cheese and bun and serve hot.

The Pork Taquitos

Total Time: 10 minutes
Servings: 5

Ingredients

- 30 oz. of cooked shredded pork tenderloin
- 2 and 1/2 cups fat free shredded mozzarella
- 10 small flour tortillas
- 1 lime (juiced)
- Cooking spray

Optional

- Salsa for dipping
- Sour Cream

Instructions

1. Preheat airfryer to 380 degrees.
2. Mix pork and lime juice well.
3. Take 5 tortillas at a time with a damp paper towel over it and microwave for 10 seconds, to soften.
4. Add 3 oz. of pork and 1/4 cup of cheese to each tortilla.
5. Roll up the tortillas compactly.
6. Organize tortillas on a greased foil lined pan.
7. Spray cooking spray over tortillas evenly.
8. Air Fry for 7-10 minutes till tortillas are a golden color, flipping half way through.
9. Serve 2 taquitos per serving.

Stromboli

Total Time: 15 minutes
Servings: 4

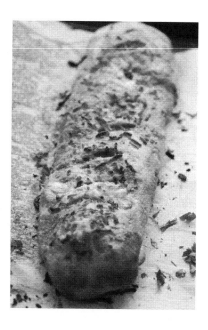

Ingredients

- 12 ounce pizza crust, refrigerated.
- 3 cup cheddar cheese, shredded.
- 0.75 cup Mozzarella cheese, shredded.
- 0.33 pound cooked ham, sliced.
- 3 ounce red bell peppers, roasted.
- 1 egg yolk.
- 1 tablespoon milk.

Instructions

1. Roll the dough out until 1/4 inch thick.
2. Layer the ham, cheese and peppers on one side of the dough. Fold over to seal.
3. Mix the egg and milk together and brush the dough.
4. Place the Stromboli into the Fry Basket and place it into the Power Air Fryer XL.
5. Press the M Button. Scroll to the Chicken Icon.
6. Press the Power Button & adjust cooking time to 15 minutes at 360 degrees.
7. Every 5 minutes, carefully flip Stromboli over.
8. Serve hot.

Air-Fried Meatloaf

Total Time: 23 minutes
Serves: 2

Ingredients

- 1 pound lean ground beef (93% fat free), raw – 15 Smart Points
- ½ medium onion, chopped – 0 SP
- 1/3c Kellog's corn flakes crumbs – 3 SP
- 1-2 tsp salt – 0SP
- 1-2 tsp freshly ground black pepper – 0 SP
- 1 tsp (or 2 cloves) minced garlic – 0SP
- 8 oz tomato sauce – 0SP
- 1 tsp dried basil – 0SP
- 5 tbsp Heinz reduced-sugar ketchup – 1SP
- 3 tsp Splenda (or Truvia) brown sugar blend – 3 SP
- 1 tbsp Worcestershire sauce – 1 SP
- ½ tbsp lightly dried (or fresh chopped) Parsley – 0SP

Instructions

1. Chop onion to desired size
2. Combine ground beef, onion, corn flakes crumbs, salt, pepper, garlic and about 6oz of the tomato sauce (save other 2oz for the glaze).
3. Mix well (by hand is best to really combine all the ingredients).
4. Take your mini loaf pans if using pans and use paper towel to lightly coat the inside with oil.
5. Split your meat mixture into two, and then place into loaf pans.
6. Make your glaze by combining the 2oz of tomato sauce, reduced-sugar ketchup, brown sugar blend, and Worcestershire sauce.
7. Brush the glaze on top and on the sides of your meatloaves.
8. Place loaves into your preheated air fryer.
9. Air fry at 360 degrees for 20 minutes, pausing twice through cooking to re-glaze the loaves (this will give great flavor as well as moisten the tops of your loaves to prevent burning from the air fryer's heating element).
10. Remove loaves from air fryer and immediately sprinkle the chopped parsley on top.
11. Let cool for a few minutes before removing from silicone pans.
12. Based on my calculations, ½ of a loaf is 6 smart points. This would go great with some mashed potatoes. Enjoy!

Taco Bell Air Fryer Crunch Wraps

Prep Time: 15 minutes | Cook Time: 4 minutes | Total Time: 19 minutes
Servings: 6

Ingredients

- 2 lbs of ground beef
- 2 packets of taco seasoning
- 1 & 1/3 cup of water
- 6 flour tortillas (12 inch)
- 3 Roma tomatoes
- 12 oz of nacho cheese
- 2 cups lettuce shredded
- 2 cups Mexican blend cheese
- 2 cups sour cream
- 6 tostadas
- Olive oil or butter spray

Instructions

1. Preheat air fryer to 400c.
2. Prepare your ground beef according to the taco seasoning packet
3. Stuff each flour tortilla with 2/3 c of beef, 4 table spoon of nacho cheese, 1 tostada, 1/3 c sour cream, 1/3 c of lettuce. 1/6th of the tomatoes and 1/3 c cheese
4. To close the tortillas flood the edges up over the center. It should look sort of a pinwheel
5. Repeat number 2 and 3 steps with remaining wraps
6. Place folded side down in your air fryer
7. Spray with oil
8. Airfry for 2 minutes or until brown
9. Carefully flip and spray again
10. Cook additional 2 minutes and repeat with remaining wraps
11. Take the time to cool it down and enjoy.

Country Fried Steak

Total Time: 15 minutes
Servings: 1

Ingredients

- 6 ounce sirloin steak (pounded thin)
- 3 eggs (beaten)
- 1 cup of flour
- 1 cup of Panko
- 1 teaspoon of onion powder
- 1 teaspoon of Garlic powder
- 1 teaspoon of salt
- 1 teaspoon of pepper
- 6 ounce ground sausage meat
- 2 tablespoons of flour
- 2 cup milk
- 1 teaspoon of pepper

Instructions

1. Mix the panko with all the spices.
2. Dredge the steak in Flour first. Then in egg, and after that in seasoned panko.
3. Place the breaded steak into the basket of the AirFryer. Fry at 370 F. Set the time for 12 minutes.
4. Once done, remove the steak from Airfryer. Serve with mashed potatoes and sausage gravy.

Sausage Gravy

5. Cook the sausage until well done. Drain the fat in it reserving 2 tbsp in the pan.
6. Add in flour to the pan with sausage, mix till all the flour is evenly mixed.
7. Add the milk slowly. Stir over a medium heat till the milk thickens.
8. Add pepper and cook for 3 more minutes to cook out the flour. Serve.

Air Fryer Chinese Salt & Pepper Pork Chops

Prep Time: 10 minutes | Cook Time: 15 minutes | Total Time: 25 minutes
Servings: 2

Ingredients

- Pork Chops
- 1 Egg White
- 1/2 teaspoon of Sea Salt
- 1/4 teaspoon of Freshly Ground Black Pepper
- 3/4 cup of Potato Starch (or cornstarch)
- 1 Oil Mister

Stir Fry

- 2 Jalapeño Pepper stems (removed, sliced)
- 2 Scallions (Green Onions) trimmes, sliced
- 2 Tablespoons of Canola Oil (or peanut)
- 1 teaspoon of Sea Salt
- 1/4 teaspoon of Freshly Ground Black Pepper
- Cast Iron Chicken Fryer

Instructions

1. Spray Air Fryer Basket with a thin coat of Oil.
2. Take a medium bowl and whisk together egg white, salt and pepper until foamy in it. Slice pork chops into cutlet pieces (leaving a little on the bones) and pat dry. Coat pork chop pieces to egg white mixture. Coat thoroughly. Marinate for at least 20 minutes.
3. Take pork chops in a large bowl and add Potato Starch. Dredge the pork chops through the Potato Starch thoroughly. Shake off excess mixture from pork and place into oil coated Air Fryer Basket. Spray pork with little Oil.
4. Cook at 360 degrees for 9 minutes. Shake the basket often and spray with oil between shakes. Cook for extra 6 minutes at 400 degrees or till the pork is brown and crispy.

Stir Fry

1. Slice Jalapeños thinly and remove the seeds from inside. Chop scallions. Take in bowl and set aside.
2. Heat wok or skillet until extremely hot. Add Jalapeño peppers, Scallions, salt, oil and pepper and stir fry approximately for a minute.
3. Add air fried pork pieces to the wok or skillet and mix them with the Jalapeño and Scallions. Stir Fry pork for an extra minute. Make sure they are fully coated with the hot oil and vegetables.

Air Fryer Sushi Roll

Prep Time: 1 hour 10 minutes | Cook Time: 10 minutes | Total Time: 1 hour 20 minutes
Servings: 3

Ingredients

For the Kale Salad

- 1 & 1/2 cups chopped kale ribs removed
- 1/2 teaspoon of rice vinegar
- 3/4 teaspoon of toasted sesame oil
- 1/8 teaspoon of garlic powder
- 1/4 teaspoon of ground ginger
- 3/4 teaspoon of soy sauce
- 1 tablespoon sesame seeds toasted (If you like)

For the Kale Salad Sushi Rolls

- 1 batch Pressure Cooker cooked Sushi Rice cooled to room temperature
- 3 sheets of sushi nori
- 1/2 of a Haas avocado sliced

Make the Sriracha Mayo

- 1/4 cup of your favorite vegan mayonnaise.

- Sriracha sauce

For the Coating

- 1/2 cup of panko breadcrumbs

Instructions

Make the Kale Salad

Take a large bowl and in it combine the kale, vinegar, sesame oil, garlic powder, ground ginger, and soy sauce. With sanitized hands, massage the kale till it turns bright green and wilted. Stir in the sesame seeds. Set them aside.

Make the Kale Salad Sushi Rolls

1. Place a sheet of nori on a dry surface. Grab a handful of rice with slightly damp fingers, and spread it onto the nori. The idea here is to make a thin layer of rice covering almost the entire nori sheet. Along one edge, leave about 1/2" of naked seaweed. This will be the flap that will seal your roll shut.
2. On the end of the seaweed opposite that naked part, add about 2-3 tablespoons of kale salad, and place a couple of slices of avocado. Roll up your sushi starting on the end of the filling by pressing gently to get a nice, tight roll. When you are close to the end, use that naked bit of seaweed to seal the roll closed. Get your fingertips wet, and moisten that bit of seaweed to make it stick if needed.
3. Repeat steps 2 to make 3 more sushi rolls.

Make the Sriracha Mayo

In a shallow bowl, whisk the vegan mayo with sriracha, till you reach the heat level that you like. Start with 1 teaspoon, and add more, 1/2 teaspoon at a time, until you have the spicy mayo according to your taste.

Fry and Slice

1. Place the panko breadcrumbs into a shallow bowl.
2. Take your first sushi roll, and coat it as evenly as possible in the Sriracha Mayo, after that in the panko. Place the roll into your air fryer basket. Repeat with the rest of your sushi rolls.
3. Fry at 390F for 10 minutes, gently shake after 5 minutes.
4. Let the rolls get cooled down. Then grab a sharp knife, and gently slice the roll into 6-8 pieces. When you're slicing don't press hard with your knife. That will just pressure kale and avocado out of the ends of your roll.
5. Serve with soy sauce.

Air-Fried Salmon Patties

Total Time: 35 minutes
Serving size: 6-8 patties

Ingredients

- 3 large russet potatoes (about 400g total)
- 1 salmon portion (about 200g)
- Frozen vegetables (parboiled and drained)
- Chopped parsley
- 2 sprinkles of dill
- Black pepper
- Salt
- 1 egg
- Breadcrumbs to coat
- Olive oil spray

Instructions

1. Chop peeled potatoes into small pieces. Cook potatoes for about 10 minutes in boiled water or until tender. Remove water and then return potatoes to the pot on low flame. Wait 2-3 minutes to let the water evaporated. Take care that the potatoes do not burn. Mash the potatoes and transfer to a large mixing bowl. Refrigerate until cooled down.
2. In the meantime, prepare your breadcrumbs if you are using bread.
3. Airfry the salmon. Preheat airfryer for 5 minutes at 180C. Then grill salmon for 5 minutes. Flake with a fork.
4. Take mash potatoes out of fridge and add parboiled vegetables, flaked salmon, chopped parsley, black pepper, dill and salt. Taste and adjust seasonings to your liking. Add the egg and combine everything together.
5. With dry sanitized hands, shape into 6-8 patties or smaller balls. Coat them with breadcrumbs, spray some oil (make sure the breadcrumbs get oil so that they can be fried well), and fry at 180C till golden (about 10-12 minutes). Flip halfway once the top is golden.
6. Serve with mayo and lemon. You can add salad as side dish.

Air-Fried Shrimp

Total Time: 15 minutes
Serves: 1

Ingredients

- Raw Shrimp (peeled)
- Fish Fry
- Yellow Mustard
- Tony's Chachere
- Cooking Spray or Olive Oil Mist

Instructions

1. Peel off shrimp and place in a plate. Sprinkle with Tony's Chachere or your preferred seasoning (keep in mind that you are not using oil, so you could use a little less seasoning than you normally would). Cover shrimp with mustard then mix all together to coat well.
2. Take fish fry in a small zip loc bag and place a few shrimp (about 5-6) in the fish fry. Close the bag and shake well to coat all over the shrimps. Repeat the process for all of your shrimps. Place the shrimp (separately, so that they don't cover each other) in the air fryer basket (will probably take about 15 or so at a time depending on the size). Spray with cooking spray or with olive oil mist to coat the fish fry.
3. Place basket into fryer and put the fryer on 330 degrees. Fry for 8 minutes. Flip your shrimp and spray again. Then put back in fryer on 330 for 7 minutes. Shrimp should be cooked nice and crispy. (Tips: If your first 8 minute side still has a good bit of dried fish fry, spray again before flipping).

3-Ingredient Fried Catfish

Prep Time: 5 minutes | Cook Time: 1 hour | Total Time: 1 hour 5 minutes
Servings: 4

Ingredients

- 4 pieces of catfish fillets
- 1/4 cup seasoned fish fry (Louisiana is used here)
- 1 tablespoon of olive oil
- 1 tablespoon of chopped parsley (optional)

Instructions

1. Preheat Air Fryer. Temperature should be 400 degrees.
2. Clean the catfish and pat dry.
3. Pour fish fry seasoning in a large Ziploc bag.
4. Place the catfish to the bag, one at a time. Seal the bag and mix well. Ensure the entire filet is coated with seasoning.
5. Spray olive oil on each filet covering the top.
6. Place the filet in the Air Fryer basket. (One at a time or according to the capacity of your basket). Cook for 10 minutes.
7. After flipping the fish cook for an additional 10 minutes.
8. Flip again.
9. Cook for another 2-3 minutes or until desired crispness.
10. Top with parsley and serve.

Spicy Fish Street Tacos with Sriracha Slaw

Total Time: 30 minutes
Serves: 2-3

Ingredients

Sriracha Slaw

- ½ cup mayonnaise
- 2 tablespoons of rice vinegar
- 1 teaspoon of sugar
- 2 tablespoons of sriracha chili sauce
- 5 cups shredded of green cabbage
- ¼ cup shredded of carrots
- 2 scallions (chopped)
- Salt
- Freshly ground black pepper

Tacos

- ½ cup flour
- 1 teaspoon of chili powder
- ½ teaspoon of ground cumin
- 1 teaspoon of salt
- Freshly ground black pepper
- ½ teaspoon of baking powder
- 1 egg (beaten)
- ¼ cup milk
- 1 cup breadcrumbs
- 12 ounces of mahi-mahi or snapper fillets
- 1 tablespoon of canola or vegetable oil
- 6 flour tortillas (6 inches each)
- 1 lime (cut into wedges)

Instructions

1. Firstly, make the sriracha slaw. Mix the mayonnaise, rice vinegar, sugar, and sriracha sauce in a large bowl. Mix well and add the green cabbage, carrots, and scallions. Toss till all the vegetables are coated with the dressing and season including salt and pepper. Refrigerate the slaw till you are ready to serve the tacos.
2. Add the flour, chili powder, cumin, salt, pepper and baking powder in a bowl. Add the egg and milk and mix until the mixture is smooth. Take the breadcrumbs in shallow dish.

3. Slice fish fillets into 1-inch wide sticks, approximately 4-inches long. You probably will have about 12 fish sticks total. Dip the fish sticks into the batter mixture, coating all sides. Let the excess batter drip off the fish and after that roll them in the breadcrumbs, patting the crumbs onto all sides of the fish sticks. Place the coated fish on a plate or baking sheet till all the fish has been coated.
4. Pre-heat the air fryer. Temperature should be 400ºF.
5. Spray the fish sticks with oil on all sides. Spray the inside of the air fryer basket with oil and place the fish to the basket. Place as many sticks as you can in one layer, keeping in mind that the sticks do not touch each other. Place any remaining sticks on top, perpendicular to the first layer.
6. Fry the fish for 3 minutes. Flip the fish sticks over and fry for an additional 2 minutes.
7. During the fish is air-frying, warm the tortilla shells either in a 350ºF oven wrapped in foil or in a skillet with a little oil over medium-high heat for a couple minutes. Fold the tortillas in half and keep them warm till the remaining tortillas and fish are ready.
8. Place two pieces of the fish in each tortilla shell and top with the sriracha slaw. Squeeze the lime wedge over top and dig in.

Air-Fried Tonkatsu with Ginger Cabbage Slaw

Total Time: 30 minutes
Serves: 4

Ingredients

For the ginger cabbage slaw

- 1/2 head red or green cabbage, or a mixture, cored and shredded (about 1 lb./500 g)
- 1 carrot (peeled and shredded)
- 1-inch (2.5-cm) piece of fresh ginger (peeled and grated)
- 1 Tbsp. of minced pickled ginger
- 1 1/2 Tbsp. of rice wine vinegar
- 3 Tbsp. of Grape seed oil
- 1 1/2 tsp. of Asian sesame oil
- 1 tsp. brown sugar
- Kosher salt

For the tonkatsu

- 1 cup (5 oz./155 g) all-purpose flour
- 2 eggs
- 1 package Sesame Panko Breadcrumbs
- 1/2 tsp. kosher salt
- 1/2 tsp. freshly of ground pepper
- 2 lb. (1 kg) boneless of pork cutlets, each about 1/2 inch (12 mm) thick
- Tonkatsu sauce

Instructions

1. In a large mixing bowl, toss together the cabbage and carrot to make the slaw. In a small bowl, mix together the fresh ginger, pickled ginger, vinegar, grape seed oil, sesame oil and brown sugar. Pour the dressing over the cabbage mixture and toss. Season with salt, cover and refrigerate until ready to serve.
2. Preheat air fryer to 360°F (182°C). Preheat an oven to 200°F (95°C). Then place a wire rack on top of a baking sheet.
3. To make the tonkatsu, take the flour, eggs and sesame panko in separate shallow bowls. Add the salt and pepper into the flour. Make one pork cutlet at a time, dip a cutlet into the flour, coating it evenly and shaking off any excess flour. After that dip it into the eggs, coating it evenly and allowing the excess egg to drip off. Finally, coat with the panko mix evenly. Take to a plate and repeat with the remaining cutlets.
4. Take half of the cutlets in a single layer in the fry basket. Insert into the air fryer. Cook for 8 minutes and open the basket. Use tongs to turn the cutlets. Increase the temperature to 400°F (200°C) and cook for 5 minutes more. Transfer the cooked cutlets to the wire rack on the baking sheet and transfer to the oven to keep warm. Reduce the temperature of the air fryer to 360°F (182°C). Repeat to cook the remaining cutlets.
5. During the cooking of second batch of cutlets, drain the coleslaw, discarding the liquid.
6. Cut each cutlet into strips about 1 inch (2.5) wide, divide evenly among 4 plates and serve. Place the slaw next to the cutlets. Serve immediately with tonkatsu sauce alongside for dipping.

Honey-Glazed Salmon

Prep Time: 2 hours | Cooking Time: 14 minutes | Total Time: 2 hours 14 minutes
Serves: 1

Ingredients

- 2 pcs Salmon Fillets (about 100gm each)
- 6 tbsp Honey
- 6 tsp Soy Sauce
- 3 tsp Hon Mirin (alternatively you can use Rice Wine Vinegar)
- 1 tsp Water

Instructions

1. Mix honey, soy sauce, Hon Mirin (sweet rice wine) and water together.
2. Pour half (or some) of the mixture in a separate bowl, set aside as this will be used as sauce serve with salmon.
3. Put together the salmon and the marinade mixture. Let it marinate for at least 2 hours.
4. Pre-heat the Airfryer at 180°C.
5. Air-grilled the salmon for 8 minutes flip over halfway and continue with additional 5 minutes. Baste the salmon with the marinade mixture every 3 minutes.
6. To prepare the sauce, pour the remaining sauce in a pan and let it simmer for 1 minute.
7. Enjoy!

Coconut Shrimp with Spicy Marmalade Sauce

Prep Time: 10 minutes | Cook Time: 20 minutes | Total Time: 30 minutes
Servings: 2

Ingredients

- 8 large shrimp (with shell and deveined)
- 8 ounces of coconut milk
- 1/2 cup of shredded, sweetened coconut
- 1/2 cup of panko bread
- 1/2 teaspoon of cayenne pepper
- 1/4 teaspoon of kosher salt
- 1/4 teaspoon of fresh ground pepper
- 1/2 cup of orange marmalade
- 1 tablespoon of honey
- 1 teaspoon of mustard
- 1/4 teaspoon of hot sauce

Directions

1. Clean the shrimp well.
2. Take a small bowl and whisk the coconut milk and season with salt and pepper in it.
3. Take another small bowl, whisk together the coconut, panko, cayenne pepper, salt and pepper.
4. Dip one shrimp at a time in the coconut milk, then in the panko and after that place in the basket of the fryer. Repeat the process till all the shrimp are coated.
5. Air fry the shrimp in the fryer for 20 minutes at 350 degrees or until the shrimp are cooked through.
6. During the shrimp cooking, whisk together the marmalade, honey, mustard and hot sauce.
7. Serve immediately the shrimp with the sauce after taking out of the fryer.

Side Dishes

Air Fryer Baked Potato Recipe

Prep Time: 5 minutes | Cook Time: 35 minutes | Total time: 40 minutes
Servings: 3

Ingredients

- 3 Idaho or Russet Baking Potatoes
- 1-2 Tablespoons Olive Oil
- 1 Tablespoon Salt
- 1 Tablespoon Garlic
- 1 Teaspoon Parsley

Instructions

1. Wash your potatoes and then create air holes with a fork in the potatoes.
2. Sprinkle them with the olive oil & seasonings, then rub the seasoning evenly on the potatoes.
3. Once the potatoes are coated place them into the basket for the Air Fryer and place into the machine.
4. Cook your potatoes at 392 degrees for 35-40 minutes or until fork tender.
5. Top with your favorites. We love fresh parsley and sour cream!

Air Fryer Fries

Prep Time: 5 minutes | Cook Time: 25 minutes | Total time: 30 minutes
Servings: 2

Ingredients

- 4 Medium Potatoes
- 4 Tbsp of Olive Oil
- Salt
- Pepper

Instructions

1. Peel potatoes and cut them into fries.
2. Place them in your Air Fryer on 180c setting. Add the olive oil before.
3. Cook for two minutes and then shake them well so that one slice does not get attached with other.
4. Cook for a further 8 minutes and shake again.
5. Cook again for 15 minutes. If you don't want golden fries in which case cook for another 5 minutes on 200c.
6. Season with salt and pepper before serving.

Baked Sweet Potato

Prep Time: 5 minutes | Cook Time: 35 minutes | Total Time: 40 minutes
Serves: 3

Ingredients

- 3 sweet potatoes
- 1 tablespoon olive oil
- 1-2 teaspoons kosher salt

Instructions

1. Wash your sweet potatoes and then create air holes with a fork in the potatoes.
2. Sprinkle them with the olive oil & salt, and then rub evenly on the potatoes.
3. Once the potatoes are coated place them into the basket for the Air Fryer and place into the machine.
4. Cook your potatoes at 392 degrees for 35-40 minutes or until fork tender.
5. Enjoy!

Air-Fried Hasselback Potatoes

Prep Time: 15 minutes | Cook Time: 30 minutes | Total time: 45 minutes
Servings: 4

Ingredients

- 4 potatoes
- Olive oil, as needed
- Bacon bits, optional
- Shredded cheese, optional

Instructions

1. Depending on your preference, either peel the potatoes or leave the skins on. If using large potatoes, cut them in half.
2. Cut slits along the potatoes about 5mm apart and 6mm from the base of the potato.
3. Preheat the air fryer to 355°F (180°C). Gently brush the potatoes with olive oil and cook them in your air fryer for 15 minutes.
4. After they've cooked for 15 minutes, brush them again with oil and continue to cook for another 15 minutes or until they are cooked through.

Air Fryer French Fries

Total Time: 30 Minutes
Serves: 1

Ingredients

- Nonstick oil spray
- 1 medium potatoes (6 oz), Yukon gold or russet, properly cleaned
- 1 teaspoon of olive oil
- 1/8 teaspoon of kosher salt
- 1/8 teaspoon of garlic powder
- Fresh cracked black pepper (to taste)

Instructions

1. Preheat the air fryer 380°F. Spray oil inside basket.
2. Cut the potato lengthwise (About 1/4 inch thin slices); then cut each slice into 1/4 inch fries. (A mandolin can help).
3. Take potatoes and oil in a medium bowl. Mix with salt, garlic powder and black pepper to taste; toss to coat.
4. Place the potatoes in the basket separately; cook the potatoes for 15 minutes, turning halfway until crisp.

Air Fryer Sweet Potato Fries

Prep Time: 5 minutes | Cook Time: 15 minutes | Total time: 20 minutes
Servings: 2

Ingredients

- 300g of Sweet Potatoes
- 3 tbsp of Olive Oil
- 1 tsp of Mustard Powder
- Salt
- Pepper

Instructions

1. Peel off the sweet potatoes. Slice them into stick shape.
2. Place them in the Airfryer with 2 tablespoons of olive oil.
3. Cook for 15 minutes at 180c. Though at the half way mark give the sweet potato a shake to avoid getting stuck to the bottom and so that they are all getting the effect of the olive oil.
4. After cooking remove them from the airfryer and place them in a bowl. Add the last tablespoon of olive oil along with the seasoning and mix well.
5. Serve.

Seasoned Crispy Potato Wedges

Total Time: 30 minutes
Servings: 4

Ingredients

- 4 medium to large russet potatoes
- 1 tbsp of bacon fat
- 1 tsp of smoked paprika
- 1 tsp of chili powder
- 1 tsp of salt
- 1/2 tsp of black pepper

Instructions

1. Clean russet potatoes and cut into 8 wedges. After cutting place in a bowl to season.
2. Microwave 1 TBS of clarified bacon fat or bacon drippings for 10 seconds.
3. Add seasonings to a bowl (smoked paprika, chili powder, salt and pepper) and mix. Add in liquid bacon fat and stir to mix again.
4. Place in basket of air fryer. Fry on 400°F for approximately 18-20 minutes. Halfway through frying time, open basket and shake well. Remove and serve potato wedges.

Garlic Parmesan Roasted Potatoes

Prep Time: 20 minutes | Cook Time: 20 minutes | Total time: 40 minutes
Servings: 6

Ingredients

- ½ teaspoon basil, dried
- 5 cloves garlic, minced
- ½ teaspoon oregano, dried
- 2 tablespoons parsley leaves
- 3 pounds red potatoes
- 1 teaspoon thyme, dried
- Kosher salt and freshly ground black pepper, to taste
- 2 tablespoons olive oil
- 2 tablespoons butter, unsalted and melted
- ⅓ cup Parmesan cheese, grated

Instructions

1. Clean and cut the potatoes into quarters.
2. In a large bowl, or a large ziplock bag, put the potatoes and the rest of the ingredients and mix / shake well.
3. Place a piece of baking paper in your Air Fryer. Set it to 400°F (200°C) and cook for 18 to 20 minutes or until the potatoes are crisp and golden.

Tip: Toss the potatoes about 10 minutes into cooking so they bake evenly.

Healthy Mediterranean Vegetables in the Airfryer

Prep Time: 5 minutes | Cook Time: 20 minutes | Total time: 25 minutes
Servings: 4

Ingredients

- 50 g of Cherry Tomatoes
- 1 Large Courgette
- 1 Green Pepper
- 1 Large Parsnip
- 1 Medium Carrot
- 1 Tsp of Mixed Herbs
- 2 Tbsp of Honey
- 1 Tsp of Mustard
- 2 Tsp of Garlic Puree
- 6 Tbsp of Olive Oil
- Salt
- Pepper

Instructions

1. Slice up the courgette and green pepper and take them in the bottom of the airfryer. Peel the parsnip and dice well. Also dice carrot and add the cherry tomatoes whole.
2. Add three tablespoons of olive oil and cover them well. Cook for 15 minutes at 180c,
3. While its cooking mix up the rest of your ingredients. Take the mixture into an Airfryer safe baking dish.
4. After the vegetables are done, transfer them from the bottom of the Airfryer into the dish and shake well so that all the vegetables are covered in the marinade.
5. Mix with a little more salt and pepper and cook for 5 minutes on 200c.
6. Serve immediately.

Recipe Notes

If you are changing the vegetables, avoid cauliflower and courgette in the same dish as both of them carry a lot of water. One of my favourite alternatives is to add sweet potatoes as this tastes amazing with honey.

Air Fryer Roasted Corn

Prep Time: 5 minutes | Cook Time: 10 minutes | Total Time: 15 minutes
Servings: 4

Ingredients

- 4 fresh ears of corn
- 2 to 3 teaspoons of vegetable oil
- Salt
- Pepper

Instructions

1. Remove husks from corn, wash and dry.
2. Cut the corn to fit in your basket.
3. If you need to do so, cut the corn. Add vegetable oil over the corn.
4. Cover the corn well with the vegetable oil. Make spicy with salt and pepper but responsibly.
5. Cook at 400 degrees in an airfryer for about 10 minutes and serve.

Air-Fried Asparagus

Prep Time: 5 minutes | Cook Time: 10 minutes | Total Time: 15 minutes
Servings: 2-4

Ingredients

- 1/2 bunch of asparagus, with 2 inches of bottom trimmed off
- Avocado or Olive Oil in a sprayer or oil mister
- Himalayan salt
- Black pepper

Instructions

1. Place asparagus spears in the air-fryer basket. Cover lightly with oil. Then sprinkle with salt and a tiny bit of black pepper.
2. Place basket inside the air-fryer and bake at 400° for 10 minutes.
3. Immediately serve.

Baked Zucchini Fries

Prep Time: 10 minutes | Cook Time: 20 minutes | Total Time: 30 minutes
Servings: 2-4

Ingredients

- 3 medium zucchini sliced into sticks
- 2 large egg white
- 1/2 cup of seasoned bread crumbs
- 2 tbsp of grated Parmesan cheese
- Cooking spray
- 1/4 teaspoon of garlic powder
- Salt
- Pepper

Instructions

1. Preheat airfryer. Temperature should be 425 Degrees.
2. Place a baking sheet in the basket. Spray it with cooking spray and set aside.
3. In a small bowl, beat egg whites and season with salt and pepper.
4. Take another bowl, place breadcrumbs, garlic powder and cheese. Combine them well.
5. Dip zucchini sticks into eggs after that into bread crumb and cheese mixture. You can dip a few at a time.
6. Transfer the breaded zucchini in a single layer onto the basket and spray more cooking spray on top.
7. Air fry at 425 degrees for about 15-20 minutes, or til golden brown color is achieved.
8. Serve with Ranch or Marinara sauce for dipping.

Air-Fried Carrots with Honey

Total Time: 15 minutes
Serves: 1

Ingredients

- 2 to 3 cups of carrots, cut in 1/2 inch pieces
- 1 tablespoon olive oil
- 1 tablespoon honey tiny drizzle of soy sauce salt and pepper to taste

Instruments

1. Set air-fryer to 390 F.
2. Place the cut carrots in a bowl, add olive oil, honey and soy, toss gently to coat, trying to cover all surfaces with a bit of oil.
3. Season carrots with salt and ground black pepper and then place in the basket of your air-fryer and cook for about 12 minutes, shaking the pan every once in a while.
4. Serve right away.

Air Fryer Hamburger Hamlet's Zucchini Zircles

Prep Time: 15 minutes | Cook Time: 8 minutes | Total time: 23 minutes
Servings: 3

Ingredients

- 3 large Zucchini
- 3/4 cup of Milk
- 1/2 cup of All Purpose Flour
- 1 cup of Seasoned Dry Italian Breadcrumbs
- 1/2 cup of Powdered Sugar
- 1 cup of Hamburger Hamlet's Secret Apricot Sauce Tools
- Oil Mister
- 1 Half Cookie Sheet
- 1 Wire Baking Rack

Instructions

1. Arrange a Cookie Sheet with Paper Towels. Wash and dry Zucchini. Cut Zucchini about 1/4 inches thick (like Poker Chips) and place on lined Cookie Sheet.
2. Take three shallow bowls, placing flour in one, milk in the next and Seasoned Bread Crumbs in the third. With one dry hand, coat Zucchini in flour, shake off excess and drop into milk. Sink with a fork and then place Zucchini in the bowl with Breadcrumbs. With other dry hand, thoroughly coat Zucchini and place onto Wire Baking Rack.
3. Gently place Zucchini Zircles in prepared/greased Air Fryer Basket separating each on from other and use an Oil Mister to spray well with Oil.
4. Cook at 390 degrees for 8 minutes, flipping one-half way through carefully.
5. Remove from Air Fryer and sprinkle with Powdered Sugar.
6. Serve with Hamburger Hamlet's Secret Apricot Sauce.

Crispy Roasted Broccoli in the Air Fryer

Prep Time: 45 minutes | Cook Time: 10 minutes | Passive Time: 50 minutes
Servings: 2

Ingredients

- 500 grams of broccoli
- 2 tablespoons of yogurt
- 1 tablespoon of chickpea flour
- 1/4 teaspoon of turmeric powder
- 1/2 teaspoon of salt
- 1/2 teaspoon of red chili powder
- 1/4 teaspoon of masala chat

Instructions

1. Cut the broccoli into small florets. Soak in a bowl of water with 2 tsp salt for 30 minutes to remove any impurities or worms.
2. Take away the broccoli florets from the water. Drain well and wipe thoroughly using a kitchen towel to absorb all the moisture.
3. Mix together all the ingredients for the marinade in a bowl.
4. Dip the broccoli florets in this marinade. Cover and keep in the refrigerator for 15 minutes.
5. Preheat the airfryer at 200°C. Place the marinated florets inside. Air fry for 10 minutes.
6. Shake the basket once midway and then check after 10 minutes if golden and crisp. If not, keep for another 2-3 minutes.
7. Eat them hot.

Lemony Green Beans

Total Time: 15 minutes
Serves: 4

Ingredients

- 1 lb. green beans, washed and de-stemmed
- 1 lemon
- Pinch of salt
- Black pepper to taste
- 1/4 teaspoon oil

Instructions

1. Put green beans in air fryer.
2. Add a few squeezes of lemon.
3. Add salt and pepper.
4. Drizzle oil over top.
5. Cook in Air Fryer at 400 degrees for 10-12 minutes.
6. Enjoy!

Air Fryer Buffalo Cauliflower

Prep Time: 5 minutes | Cook Time: 15 minutes | Total time: 20 minutes
Serves: 4

Ingredients

For the Cauliflower

- 4 cups cauliflower florets (each one should be approx. the size of two baby carrots)
- 1 cup panko breadcrumbs mixed with 1 teaspoon sea salt (sea salt grains are bigger, and they add a little extra crunch to the breading)

For the Buffalo Coating

- 1/4 cup melted vegan butter
- 1/4 cup vegan Buffalo sauce

For Dipping

- vegan mayo (Cashew Ranch, or your favorite creamy salad dressing)

Instructions

1. Melt and mix the vegan butter in a mug with buffalo sauce. You can melt the butter in an microwave.
2. Holding by the stem, dip each floret in the butter/buffalo mixture for getting most of the floret coated in sauce. It is perfect if a bit of the stem doesn't get saucy. Hold the floret over the mug until it pretty much stops dripping.
3. Dredge the dipped floret in the panko/salt mixture, coating as much as you like, then place in the air fryer. Place them with any separation.
4. Do not preheat. Air fry at 350F for 14-17 minutes, shaking a few times while checking them. Your cauliflower is done when the florets are a little bit browned.
5. Serve with dipping sauce of choice.

Air Fryer Crispy Honey Garlic Chicken Wings

Prep Time: 10 minutes | Cook Time: 35 minutes | Total time: 45 minutes
Serves: 2

Ingriedents

- 16 Pieces of Chicken Wings
- 3/4 cup of Potato Starch
- 1/4 cup of Clover Honey
- 1/4 cup of Butter
- 4 Tablespoons of Fresh Garlic minced
- 1/2 teaspoon of Kosher Salt
- 1/8 cup Fresh Water (or more as needed)

Instructions

1. Clean chicken wings appropriately. Take Potato Starch to bowl and coat chicken wings. Place coated chicken wings to Air Fryer.
2. Cook at 380 degrees for 25 minutes, shaking the basket every five minutes during cooking.
3. Cook at 400 degrees for another 5-10 minutes. All skin on all wings should be very dry and crisp.
4. Heat a small stainless steel saucepan on low heat. Melt butter and then add garlic. Let the garlic be there in heat for 5 minutes.
5. Add honey and salt and simmer on low for about 20 minutes, stirring every few minutes, keeping in mind that the sauce should not burn. Add a few drops of water after 15 minutes to keep Sauce away from hardening.
6. Remove chicken wings from Air Fryer and pour over the sauce.

Air Fryer Party Meatballs

Prep Time: 20 minutes | Cook Time: 15 minutes | Total Time: 35 minutes
Servings: 24

Ingredients

- 1 lb Mince Beef
- ¾ Cup Tomato Ketchup
- 1 Tbsp Tabasco
- 2 1/2 Tbsp Worcester Sauce
- ¼ Cup Vinegar
- 1 Tbsp Lemon Juice
- ½ Cup Brown Sugar
- ½ Tsp Dry Mustard
- 3 Gingersnaps crushed

Instructions

1. In a large mixing bowl place on your seasonings and mix well so that everything is evenly coated.
2. Add the mince to the bowl and mix well.
3. Form into medium sized meatballs and place them into your Air Fryer.
4. Cook them for 15 minutes on a 190c heat or until nice and crispy and cooked in the middle.
5. Place them on sticks before serving.

Recipe Notes

When I am cooking in the Air Fryer I find that it doesn't do a very good job if the contents are overcrowded, so if you have a small Air Fryer I suggest you do them in batches of 12.

Air Fryer Pressure Cooker Honey Bourbon Chicken Wings

Prep Time: 10 minutes | Cook Time: 22 minutes | Total Time: 32 minutes
Servings: 4

Ingredients

- 3-5 pounds of Chicken Wing Parts
- 3/4 cup of Heinz Ketchup
- 1 Tablespoon of Liquid Smoke
- 1/2 cup of Light Brown Sugar
- 1/4 cup of Onions finely minced
- 2 cloves of Fresh Garlic finely crushed
- 1/2 cup of Fresh Water
- 1/4 cup of Bourbon
- 2 teaspoons of Smoked Paprika
- 1/4 teaspoon of Cayenne Pepper
- 3 Tablespoons of Clover Honey
- 1 teaspoon of Sea Salt
- 1/2 teaspoon of Freshly Ground Black Pepper

Instructions

1. Push the Sauté or Browning button on your Pressure Cooker.
2. Place ketchup, liquid smoke, brown sugar, onion and garlic to your Pressure Cooker cooking pot.
3. Stir until sauce starts to thicken, about 5 minutes.
4. Turn Pressure Cooker off.
5. Place the water and the rest of the ingredients.
6. Add the wings and mix into the sauce.
7. Lock on the lid and Close the Pressure Valve.
8. Cook on High Pressure for 5 minutes straight.
9. When it sounds beep, do a Quick Release.
10. Gently remove wings from the Pressure Cooker and take into the Air Fryer Basket.
11. Turn the Pressure Cooker to Sauté or Browning and allow sauce to thicken while the wings are crisping in the airfryer.
12. Place basket into airfryer and set temperature to 400 degrees Fahrenheit for 6 minutes.
13. Remove the basket from the air fryer and dunk wings into the sauce. Mix well.
14. Take the wings to the Air Fryer and set temperature to 400 degrees Fahrenheit for 6 minutes.
15. Serve with extra sauce for dipping.

Air Fryer Baked Thai Peanut Chicken Egg Rolls

Prep Time: 10 minutes | Cook Time: 8 minutes | Total time: 18 minutes
Serves: 4

Ingredients

- 4 egg roll wrappers
- 2 c. rotisserie chicken (shredded)
- ¼ c. Thai peanut sauce
- 1 medium carrot (very thinly sliced)
- 3 green onions (chopped)
- ¼ red bell pepper (julienned)
- non-stick cooking spray or sesame oil

Instructions

1. Preheat Airfryer to 390°.
2. In a small bowl, mix the chicken with the Thai peanut sauce.
3. Lay the egg roll wrappers on a clean dry surface. Over the bottom third of an egg roll wrapper, place ¼ the carrot, bell pepper and onions. Add ½ cup of the chicken mixture over the vegetables.
4. Moisten the outside edges of the wrapper with water. Fold the sides of the wrapper toward the center and roll tightly so that the fillers do not come out.
5. Repeat the process with remaining wrappers. (Keep remaining wrappers covered with a damp paper towel till ready to use.)
6. Spray the egg rolls with non-stick cooking spray. Turn the rolls over and spray the back sides as well.
7. Place the egg rolls in the Airfryer and bake at 390° for 6-8 minutes (Till they are crispy and golden brown.)
8. Slice in half and serve with Thai Peanut Sauce for dipping.

Air Fryer Parmesan Dill Fried Pickle Chips

Prep Time: 14 minutes | Cook Time: 16 minutes | Total Time: 30 minutes
Serves: 4

Ingredients

- 32 oz. jar of whole large dill pickles
- 2 eggs
- ⅔ c. of panko bread crumbs
- ⅓ c. of grated Parmesan
- ¼ tsp. of dried dill weed

Instructions

1. Slice the large pickles diagonally into approximately ¼" thick slices. Pat dry by place between layers of paper towels.
2. Take a shallow bowl, beat the eggs until smooth. Take a resalable bag. In it add the Panko bread crumbs, Parmesan and dill weed and shake until well combined.
3. In batches of 4-5 pieces, dip the pickle slices into the egg mixture, remove any excess egg and then toss in the Panko mixture.
4. Place half of the coated pickle chips into the Airfryer and bake for 8-10 minutes on the highest temperature. Remove from the Airfryer and repeat the process for the remaining. Serve immediately with zesty ranch for dipping.

Cheeseburger Egg Rolls

Prep Time: 15 minutes | Cook Time: 25 minutes | Total Time: 40 minutes
Serves: 6

Ingredients

- 8 oz. raw extra-lean ground beef (4% fat or less)
- 1/4 tsp of garlic powder
- 1/4 tsp of onion powder
- Salt
- Black pepper
- 1/2 cup chopped bell pepper
- 1/2 cup chopped onion
- 3 tbsp of shredded reduced-fat cheddar cheese
- 3 tbsp of light/reduced-fat cream cheese
- 2 tbsp of ketchup
- 1 tbsp of yellow mustard
- 6 hamburger dill pickle chips (chopped)
- 6 large square egg roll wrappers
- Optional dips: additional ketchup and yellow mustard

Instructions

1. Take a large skillet sprayed with nonstick spray to medium-high heat. Place beef, and sprinkle with seasonings. Add bell pepper and onion. Cook and stir until beef is fully cooked and veggies have softened. It will take about 5 minutes.
2. Take away skillet from heat, and add cheddar cheese, cream cheese, ketchup, and mustard. Stir until thoroughly mixed and melted.
3. Place mixture to a medium-large bowl. Fold in chopped pickles.
4. Lay an egg roll wrapper flat on a dry and clean surface. Distribute evenly about 1/6th of the mixture (about 1/3 cup) in a row a little below the center. Moisten all four edges by dabbing your fingers in water and going over the edges smoothly. Grab the sides and fold about 3/4 inches toward the middle, to keep mixture from falling out. Roll up the wrapper around the mixture and continue to the top. Seal the top with a dab of water.
5. Repeat to make more egg rolls.
6. Spray the rolls with nonstick spray.
7. Place one batch in the air fryer cooking basket in a single layer.
8. Air fry at 392 degrees for 7-9 minutes or until golden brown.
9. Serve hot.

Air-Fried Homemade Potato Chips

Prep Time: 5 minutes | Cook Time: 22 minutes | Total time: 27 minutes
Serves: 1

Ingredients

- 2 medium russet potatoes (scrubbed)
- ½ Tsp of Extra Virgin Olive Oil
- salt to taste

Instructions

1. Clean the potatoes and slice them thinly. The easiest and most uniform way to do this is with a mandolin, but you can use a knife, also.
2. Soak slices in a bowl of cold water for 30 minutes; change the water halfway through.
3. Spread potatoes out on paper towels and blot dry.
4. Toss potatoes with ½ tablespoon of extra virgin olive oil, plus a little salt.
5. Cook at 392 degrees for approximately 22 minutes.
6. After taking out of the airfryer add more salt or other seasonings to taste.

Air-Fry Corn Tortilla Chips Recipe

Prep Time: 1 minute | Cook Time: 3 minutes | Total Time: 4 minutes
Serve: 1

Ingredients

- 8 Corn Tortillas
- 1 tbsp of olive oil
- Salt to taste

Instructions

1. Preheat Airfryer. Temperature should be 200C.
2. With a sharp knife, cut corn tortillas into triangle shapes.
3. Cover the tortillas with olive oil.
4. Place half of the tortilla pieces in wire basket and airfry for 3 minutes.
5. Repeat the process for remaining batch.
6. Sprinkle with salt.
7. Serve.

Banana Chips Recipe with Air Fryer

Total time: 30 minutes
Serves: 1

Ingredientes

- Raw Banana – 3-4 pcs
- Salt – 1 tsp
- Turmeric powder – 1/2 tsp
- Chaat masala – ½ tsp
- Oil – 1 tsp

Instructions

1. Peel the bananas. Cut them into poker chips like round shape.
2. Make a mixture of water, turmeric powder and salt. Place banana slices in this mixture. It will prevent the bananas to turn black and also will give nice yellow color. Keep bananas there to soaked in this mixture for 5 -10 min. Drain the water and dry the chips.
3. Spray little oil on chips to avoid sticking of banana chips in Airfryer. Preheat the air fryer at 180 degrees for 5 min. Fry the chips for 15 min at 180 degrees. Add salt and chat masala.
4. Serve immediately.

Garlic Parmesan Oil-Free Air Fryer Chips

Prep Time: 30 minutes | Cook Time: 30 minutes | Total Time: 60 minutes
Serves: 1

Ingredients

- 2 Large Red Potatoes
- 2 tsp of salt
- 4 garlic cloves (crushed or minced)
- 2 tbsp of homemade vegan parmesan

Instructions

1. Thinly slice the potatoes
2. Place the sliced potatoes in a bowl and fill with water. Add and mix 2 teaspoons of salt. Let soak for 30 minutes.
3. Drain water while rinsing the potatoes. Pat dry.
4. Toss the potatoes with crushed garlic and vegan parmesan.
5. Layer half of the potato slices in the air fryer, 4 layer maximum. Don't overload the air fryer otherwise the chips won't cook evenly.
6. Fry at 170 degrees for 20-25 minutes, or till dry to the touch and no longer flimsy. Shake the basket every 5 minutes or so.
7. Rise the temperature up to 400 degrees and fry for an additional 5 minutes or until the potatoes has become crunchy.
8. Remove from the air fryer and top with more salt.
9. Repeat the process for the other half of the potato slices.
10. Serve immediately.

Ranch Kale Chips

Prep Time: 5 minutes | Cook Time: 5 minutes | Total Time: 10 minutes
Serves: 2

Ingredients

- 2 tablespoons of olive oil
- 4 cups loosely packed kale stemmed
- 2 teaspoons of Vegan Ranch Seasoning
- 1 tablespoon of nutritional yeast flakes
- 1/4 teaspoon of salt

Instructions

1. Take the oil, kale pieces, Ranch Seasoning, and nutritional yeast and mix together in a medium-sized bowl. After that place the mixed kale into the basket of your air fryer.
2. Airfry at 370 for 4-5 minutes (Without preheating), shake after halfway done.
3. Immediate serve.

Ranch Seasoned Air Fryer Chickpeas

Prep Time: 5 minutes | Cook Time: 20 minutes | Total Time: 25 minutes
Serves: 4

Ingredients

- 1 15 ounce can chickpeas (drained but NOT rinsed)
- 2 tablespoons of olive oil (divided)
- 1 batch Homemade Ranch Seasoning
- 1 teaspoon of sea salt
- 2 tablespoons of lemon juice

Instructions

1. Take a small bowl and toss together the chickpeas and 1 tablespoon of the olive oil in it.
2. Air fry at 400F for 15 minutes.
3. Transfer the chickpeas back to the small bowl, and sprinkle with the remaining oil plus the Ranch Seasoning, salt, and lemon juice so the beans get nice and coated.
4. Place the chickpeas back to your air fryer basket and cook at 350F for 5 more minutes
5. Serve immediately, or cool completely and then store in an airtight container.

Air Fryer Apple Chips

Prep Time: 4 minutes | Cook Time: 8 minutes | Total Time: 12 minutes
Servings: 1

Ingredients

- 1 medium apple
- ¼ tsp cinnamon
- ¼ tsp nutmeg

Instructions

1. Preheat Air Fryer. Temperature should be 375° F.
2. Slice apple very thinly using a mandolin or a knife.
3. Take a bowl and mix together apple slices, cinnamon and nutmeg in it.
4. Place seasoned apple slices to air fryer basket in one layer.
5. Bake for 8 minutes, flip while halfway.
6. Serve hot.

Air-Baked Molten Lava Cake

Total time: 20 minutes
Serves: 4

Ingredients

- 1.5 TBS Self Rising Flour
- TBS of Baker's Sugar (Not Powdered)
- OZ of Unsalted Butter
- OZ of Dark Chocolate (Pieces or Chopped)
- 2 Eggs

Instructions

1. Preheat Air Fryer to 375F.
2. Take 4 standard oven safe ramekins. Grease and flour them.
3. Melt dark chocolate and butter in a microwave safe bowl on level 7 for 3 minutes, stir occasionally. Remove from microwave and stir till it has even consistency.
4. Whisk the eggs and sugar till the mixture gets pale and frothy.
5. Include melted chocolate mixture into egg mixture. Stir in flour. Use a spatula to combine everything evenly.
6. Fill the ramekins about 3/4 full with cake mixture. Bake in preheated air fryer. Temperature is 375F and time 10 minutes.
7. Remove from the air fryer and allow cooling for 2 minutes. Carefully turn ramekins upside down onto serving plate. Tap the bottom with a butter knife to loosen edges. Cake should release from ramekin with little effort and center should appear dark and gooey. Enjoy with or without a raspberry drizzle.

Air Fryer Apple Dumplings

Cooking Time: 25 minutes | Cooling Time: 10 minutes | Total Time: 60 minutes
Servings: 2

Ingredients

- 2 very small apples
- 2 tablespoons raisins or sultanas
- 1 tablespoon brown sugar
- 2 sheets puff pastry
- 2 tablespoons butter, melted

Instructions

1. Preheat your air fryer to 356°F.
2. Core and peel the apples.
3. Mix the raisins or sultanas and the brown sugar together in a bowl.
4. Put each apple on 1 of the puff pastry sheets then fill the core with the raisins or sultanas and sugar mixture.
5. Fold the pastry around the apple so it is fully covered.
6. Place the apple dumplings on a small sheet of foil, so if any juices escape they don't fall into the air fryer.
7. Brush the dough with the melted butter.
8. Place in your air fryer and set the timer for 25 minutes and bake the apple dumplings until golden brown and the apples are soft.
9. Turn the apples over once during cooking so that they will cook evenly.
10. Let cool for 10 minutes.
11. Serve with ice cream if desired.

Air Fryer Five Cheese Pull Apart Bread

Prep Time: 15 minutes | Cook Time: 4 minutes | Total Time: 19 minutes
Servings: 2

Ingredients

- 1 Large Bread Loaf
- 100g Butter
- 2 Tsp of Garlic Puree
- 30g of Cheddar Cheese
- 30g of Goats Cheese
- 30g of Mozzarella Cheese
- 30g of Soft Cheese
- 30g of Edam Cheese
- 2 Tsp of Chives
- Salt
- Pepper

Instructions

1. Grate your hard cheese into four different piles.
2. Melt the butter in a pan on a medium heat. Mix the chives, salt and pepper and the garlic. Cook for another 2 minutes and mix well.
3. Make little slits into your bread with a good knife. In each of the little slit wholes cover with garlic butter until you have done them all. After that cover them all with soft cheese to give them a lovely creamy taste.
4. In every other one place a little cheddar and a little goats' cheese.
5. The final ones that have not been filled add the Edam and mozzarella.
6. Place in the Air Fryer for 4 minutes or until the cheese is melted and the bread warm.
7. Serve.

Recipe Notes

Use soft bread so that if does not get hard while cooking.

5-Ingredient Air Fryer Chocolate Mug Cake

Prep Time: 2 minutes | Cook Time: 10 minutes | Total time: 12 minutes
Serves: 1

Ingredients

- ¼ Cup of Self Raising Flour
- 5 Tbsp of Caster Sugar
- 1 Tbsp of Cocoa Powder
- 3 Tbsp of Whole Milk
- 3 Tsp of Coconut Oil

Instructions

1. Mix all the ingredients together in the mug. Make the mixture even all around.
2. Place the mug in the Airfryer. Cook for 10 minutes at 200c. Repeat with other cups with the mixture.
3. Serve!

Note: The time may vary depending on whether you like it runny like a lava cake or if you like it more stiff like a traditional chocolate cake. For runny go for 10 minutes, a little melted chocolate centre for 13 minutes and 17 minutes for the traditional chocolate cake in a mug.

Air Fryer Pizza Hut Bread Sticks

Prep Time: 10 minutes | Cook Time: 15 minutes | Total Time: 25 minutes
Servings: 4

Ingredients

- 1/3 Homemade Pizza Dough
- 2 Tbsp of Desiccated Coconut
- 1 Tsp of Garlic Puree
- 25g of Cheddar Cheese
- Bread Seeds optional
- 1 Tsp of Parsley
- Salt
- Pepper

Instructions

1. Melt your coconut oil in a small pan. Add your seasoning and your garlic puree and mix well.
2. Take your pizza dough and cut into a thick rectangular shape. Cover it with your garlic oil until it is all evenly coated. Cover garlic oil with desiccated coconut on the top.
3. Add some of cheddar cheese and then finish with some bread seeds.
4. Cook in the Airfryer for 10 minutes at 180c. Another 5 minutes at 200c or until hot in the middle and nice and crispy on the outside.
5. Chop into fingers shape and serve.

Fruit Crumble Mug Cakes

Prep Time: 15 minutes | Cook Time: 15 minutes | Total time: 30 minutes
Servings: 4

Ingredients

- 110g Plain Flour
- 50g Butter
- 30g Caster Sugar
- 30g Gluten Free Oats
- 25g Brown Sugar
- 4 Plums
- 1 Small Apple
- 1 Small Pear
- 1 Small Peach
- Handful Blueberries
- 1 Tbsp Honey

Instructions

1. Preheat the Air Fryer. The temperature should be 160c.
2. Remove the cores and the stones from the fruit. Dice into very small decorative pieces.
3. Place the fruit in the bottom of the mugs. Sprinkle with brown sugar and honey until all the fruit is well covered.
4. Place the flour, butter and caster sugar into a mixing bowl. Rub the fat into the flour. When it shows fine breadcrumbs, add the oats and mix well.
5. Cover the tops of the mugs with a layer of the crumble.
6. First place in the Air Fryer for 10 minutes at 160c. Then cook for a further 5 minutes at 200c so that you can get crunch to the top of your crumble.

Parmesan Dusted Garlic Knots

Prep Time: 10 minutes | Cook Time: 4 minutes | Total Time: 14 Minutes
Serves: 1

Ingredients

- 1 13.8 Oz Refrigerated Pizza Crust
- 3 Tbsp Olive Oil
- 3 Tbsp Minced Garlic
- Garlic Salt
- Parmesan Cheese Powder

Instructions

1. Roll dough out onto cutting board. Cut them into equal one fourth strips.
2. Wrap each strip by making knots.
3. Take Olive Oil & Garlic in a bowl and mix. Dip the knots into the mixture
4. Place them on a plate and dash with Garlic Salt.
5. Transfer 12 balls at a time to Air Fryer.
6. Set Fryer for 400° for 4 minutes (please note, more batches will need less time, so you will probably end up at about 2minutes per batch rather than 4 minutes)
7. Once timer stops, open, remove to platter, and serve with Parmesan.
8. An approximate of 38 pieces will be made.

Super Soft Air Fryer Chocolate Chip Cookies

Prep Time: 5 minutes | Cook Time: 8 minutes | Total Time: 13 minutes
Serves: 9

Ingredients

- 100g of Butter
- 75g of Brown Sugar
- 175g of Self Raising Flour
- 100g of Chocolate
- 2 Tbsp of Honey
- 1 Tbsp of Milk

Instructions

1. Preheat the airfryer. Set it to 180c.
2. In a large bowl beat the butter until soft. Then add the sugar and cream them together. Until the mixture becomes fluffy.
3. Add the honey and flour and mix well.
4. Smash up your chocolate so that they are a mix of medium and really small chocolate chunks.
5. Add chocolate to the mix.
6. And milk and make the mixture even.
7. Place the cookies into the airfryer on a baking sheet and cook for six minutes at 180c. Then reduce the temperature to 160c for a further 2 minutes so that they can cook in the middle.
8. Enjoy.

Conclusion

We all are fan of good food. It's not just our fuel, it's our mood manipulator. We all know how important it is to eat healthy when we are so hungry that we forget what healthy is. We often eat what we find most accessible. So why not make the good things most easy to have. I know things not always go as we expect. You will always find other attractions. But from now I believe you can trust on this book to overcome those others as you know you can make that same thing healthier with the least possible time. I definitely am not bragging about it. Many chief has confirmed that an air fryer can make it healthier and quicker. This is even not an alternative of oven; it is unique by its own in the sense of through cooking. There are a lot of recipes that we have now and I guess it will help us experiment a bit deeper with our taste. It is also something to trust on while on vacation. As it always cook the food thoroughly; so you can depend on this when you are relaxing in a recreational vehicle with your favorite music on. For all these and a lot of unspoken reasons my confidence is on the air fryer and the taste that the recipes will serve. I will be very happy to know your honest opinions. Reviews are always the motivation for next work. Please let me know what you think. Live healthy, live strong.

Made in the USA
San Bernardino, CA
24 October 2018